LANCASTER AS IT WAS

by Kenneth Docton

Cover picture: Market Street and Town Hall, c. 1850, Lithograph by E. H. Buckler.
(courtesy of Lancaster Museum).

Published by Hendon Publishing Co. Ltd., Hendon Mill, Nelson.
Text © Kenneth Docton. 1973
Printed by: Fretwell & Brian Ltd., Howden Hall, Silsden, Nr. Keighley, Yorkshire.

42p

INTRODUCTION

WHEN people mention "Time Honoured Lancaster" they envisage buildings of the Tudor period, buildings of half timber construction as those to be seen at Chester, or they may hope to see paintings and water colours of that type of building which no longer exist, and which in my opinion never existed. Such records of Preston can be seen in the Harris Institute but so far as I know Lancaster was never like that.

Before the development of Lancaster as a port by the West India Trade, in the middle of the 18th century, it seems that the standard of the buildings was very low. In the 1690's Celia Fiennes who revisited the town said that it "was old and much decay'd and in 1698 there was a great fire which destroyed many wooden buildings on the north side of Church Street (Autobiography of William Stout). So that when we look at Lancaster between say 1790-1890 we find a mixture of good Georgian buildings erected by the Merchants and those who prospered by their trade, some public buildings, and the cramped dwellings of the working classes in the back streets and alleys of the town, some of these being the renovated shacks of the days of the merchants and others of the period of the Industrial Revolution. But Tudor, none.

Some of these are shown in this book as they then existed, while others still remain. Other subjects are worthy of inclusion but time and cost limit what can be done. I wish to acknowledge with thanks the assistance given to me in the preparation of this book by Mrs. E. Tyson, Curator of the Lancaster Museum and Mr. E. H. Lowe, City Librarian and his assistant Miss Walmsley.

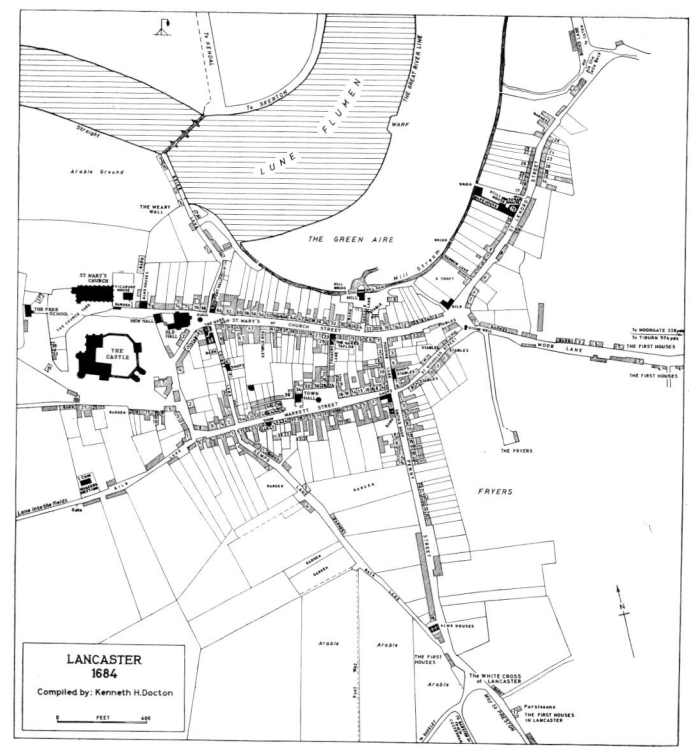

Docton's Map of 1684

This is the oldest detailed map of Lancaster. It was compiled from crumpled up sheets of a survey of the town found, in 1952, in the basement of Towneley Hall, Burnley. The name of the surveyor is not known, but the survey can be dated as the mayor is shown by name as the occupant of property in Market Street.

Market Square about 1880, showing the premises of T. Satterthwaite, Wine Merchants; Richardson, surgeon; and those once occupied by J. P. Rowlandson, hairdresser who had moved to 57, Market Street. On the right hand side are the offices of the Gas Company which was transferred to the Corporation in 1880. The dilapidated condition of the buildings in the town at this time is obvious from this photograph, but the three that follow, apart from their particular significance, show the improvement to the square.

Visit of the Duke and Duchess of York (later King George V) 24th March, 1896 to open The Royal Lancaster Infirmary. It will be observed that the premises of Mansergh & Son (now Lancaster Co-op) have replaced those occupied by T. Satterthwaite.

Market Square in the early 1900's showing the premises occupied by Lawson, Roper & Procter; W. Watson, hairdresser; Mansergh & Son; the offices (with the arched doorway) of the Borough Accountant and Rates Offices, and the square with open market stalls.

Market Square, 9th August, 1902, Coronation Day, showing the Ox Roasting. Most of the functions at this time, and for many years before, were organised by Mr. J. Sly of the King's Arms Hotel. The detail shown on this photograph is of great interest. Messrs Roper, Proctor and Harris occupied the upper floor of the building to the left; the ground floor being empty. Chancery Lane is shown along with the Gas Office, over which the Borough Accountant and Assistant Overseer had their offices. In the corner we can see Anchor Lane with John Day's Blue Anchor Hotel (the meeting place of the R.A.O.B.). Next is the shop of H. Bartle, grocer and then Bradleys Outfitters, the latter being probably the oldest premises in the town erected in main by William Stout. The police in attendance are wearing Army surplus helmets left over from the Boer War. Sergeant Johnson is standing at the entrance to Chancery Lane.

The first Lancaster Dispensary, or House of Recovery, which was demolished in 1906 to permit the extension of the Storey Institute. On part of the site was re-erected the entrance from Cawthorne House which was demolished for the erection of the General Post Office.

The recess above the doorway contained an alabaster plaque representing the Parable of the Good Samaritan. This plaque was removed to the second and third Dispensaries and then to the Royal Infirmary where it can still be seen.

The second Dispensary on Castle Hill, now occupied by Morris & Irwin, estate agents. The recess for the plaque of the Good Samaritan is over the doorway and above the plaque the word DISPENSARY can be seen very faintly.

Thurnham Street. The building behind the chimney sweep together with that adjoining was the town house of Lord Viscount Fauconberg who died in 1815. The low building was demolished and replaced by the Royal Hotel. That adjoining with the recess above the door, now the Public Health Offices, was the third Lancaster Dispensary. The building behind the lamp column at the junction with Lucy Street has been demolished and is now a Town Hall car park. The building beyond, which was the birth place of Sir Richard Owen, K.C.B., was demolished to improve the entrance to Brock Street.

Prior to 1876 the Great Gateway to Lancaster Castle was obstructed by medieaval cottages. The buildings shown here in the course of demolition were the subject of an intensive publicity campaign by Mr. Swainson, Town Clerk, whereby sufficient funds became available for the purchase and demolition of the property.

Some of the now extinct pageantry at Lancaster Castle. The arrival of the High Sheriff, H. L. Storey, in 1904.

Part of China Lane, now China Street, looking north, before it's part demolition in 1895. At the far end can be seen Church Street and on the left are the premises occupied by 'Marjee'.

A section of China Street that still exists but unfortunately the elevation has been ruined by the alteration to the ground floor. It is the premises of 'Marjee'.

Fleet Square in the early 1900's. Looking south from Cable Street.

Dalton Square before the erection of the Queen Victoria Statue. The building on the right hand side was the first purpose built Roman Catholic Church in Lancaster which later became the Palatine Hall and then the County Cinema. It is now empty, along with the dilapidated house next door which was once the residence of the notorious Dr. Ruxton. The memorial to the memory of Thomas Johnson was removed to Stonewell where it still stands. Before the erection of the statue the square had been used for various purposes including the sale of sheep and cattle, and concerts by the band of the Lancaster Militia, whose mess room was at 5, Dalton Square. It also housed one of the two small night watchmens huts, the other being in Queens Square.

Spring Garden Street B
Lancaster

Spring Garden Street looking towards King Street where the Ring O' Bells can be seen. This street has been so altered as to be unrecognisable.

The Corner of Church Street and North Road in 1892. This corner is now completely unrecognisable. The main theme seems to be LIQUOR.

Upper Church Street. The building opposite the lamp column was demolished to make the new road. That at the end of the picture was demolished for the new Masonic Hall, which was the oldest dated building, 1664, in the town. The date stone was destroyed during demolition. The building above, is the Conservative Club in which Prince Charles Edward (Bonnie Prince Charlie) resided during the 1745 rebellion.

Lower Church Street as it was in 1910.

A BIT OF OLD LANCASTER. (PENNY STREET)

Upper King Street at it's junction with Penny Street about 1900. The White Cross Hotel is at the extreme left followed by the Corporation Arms, (the stone arms are now in the Museum) then a sweet shop. The whole of this property was demolished and replaced by the present White Cross Hotel, the Farmers Arms and Loxham's Garages.

Penny Street Bridge in the late 1800's; looking down King Street. The White Cross Hotel at the junction with Aldcliffe Road is on the left.

The old Merchants News Room

The Old Merchant's News Room at the corner of King Street and Market Street, demolished in 1912. This site and the other adjoining buildings were included in a road widening scheme. The News Room was a place frequently used by the leading merchants, ship owners and gentlemen of various professions. The electric tram lines and overhead wires of the old tramway system are visible in the photograph. The premises as set back are now occupied by J. M. Wigley Ltd., booksellers.

Two photographs of Market Street, looking east, showing on the right Fenton Cawthorne House which was demolished in 1921 to make way for the General Post Office and next to it the Old Kings Arms Hotel demolished and rebuilt in 1880. The entrance portico to Cawthorne House was re-erected at the back of the Storey Institute and the side entrance now forms the back entrance on Heysham Road to one of the premises fronting Sandylands Promenade. On the left is the Commercial Temperance Hotel now demolished and replaced by a public garden.

Old King Street. The building at the far end was occupied by the Magistrates Clerk's Office and that under the notice board by Mr. Robertson, vetinary surgeon. All the buildings have been demolished and now form the site of shops and studio 1, and 2, (late Odeon).

Winder's Court, Monmouth Street.

Bridge Lane Lancaster. a

Looking down Old Bridge Lane, now demolished. This road was once the only way into and from the town over the old Lancaster Bridge.

Looking up Old Bridge Lane, now demolished. The only remaining building is the Carpenter's Arms shown on the left hand side of the photograph.

Cable Street Auction Rooms at the junction of Cable Street and Water Street, now the site of a block of modern offices erected by Mansergh & Sons.

St. Leonard's Gate. The site is now the car park to the north of the Theatre. The building with the lamp attached was the Black Cat Hotel, later the Atheneum.

Gillison's Hospital (Alms Houses) in Common Garden Street, which were demolished in 1960. The tenants were rehoused in new premises in Lindow Square. The roof of the Market Hall can be seen above the buildings.

Horse Shoe Corner, looking north, St. Nicholas Street to the right. The premises on the corner were occupied by Peter Bromley and Woods and Brown, ironmongers, smiths and grocers and shown in the 1881 directory as Woods & Bromley, Cheapside.

The start of the last occasion of Riding the Old Boundary at nine in the morning of the 4th June, 1900. The Riding in 1788 departed at 5.0 a.m. and did not return until late evening. When the custom originated is not known but it still takes place every seven years although shorn of most of its romantic trappings. The Riding of 1774 consisted of 150 horsemen followed on foot by 1,500 local inhabitants. The photograph shows the old Town Hall, Fire Station, Police Station and the distributing structure for the overhead telephone lines of the National Telephone Company.

The Keep at the Bowerham Barracks erected 1876-80. It was occupied by the King's Own (Royal Lancaster) Regiment, but is now used as a library by St. Martins College.

The Opening of the Lancaster Girls Grammar School, October, 1914. With the exception of the girls most of the local dignitaries shown here are dead. At the top of the steps is Chief Constable Harris. There is also the Town Clerk, Mr. T. Cann Hughes, Mr. Briggs, Alderman Bowness, W. Jackson, Sir Noval Helme and many others easily recognisable, but I think that it may be of more interest to the girls who are still living.

Peace Celebration Procession 1918 passing up Market Street. The photograph shows the exhibit of the National Projectile Factory (shells) which were filled with explosives at the National Filling Factory, White Lund.

The Opening of Westfield War Memorial Village by Earl Haig, seated, on 27th November, 1924. The Mayor, Alderman and Councillors surround the table at which he is seated. Those taking part in this ceremony were the President Mr. H. L. Storey, the architect Mr. T. H. Mawson, the Vice President Alderman W. Briggs, and the Mayor, Alderman Jackson. The houses on this estate are named after the names of places and persons associated with the 1914-18 War.

The Locomotive "Engineer Lancaster" standing outside the former depot of the L. & N. W. R. at Brunton Road, Lancaster. It was designed in 1874 by Mr. F. W. Webb. One of this class distinguished itself in the 1895 railway races to Scotland. (Photograph by courtesy of M. J. Borrowdale).

The Lancaster Fire Brigade on 13th June, 1907 outside the Court Buildings of Lancaster Castle.
Standing on the ladder: Top, Sergeant Garth, Fireman Casse, Helme and Riley.
In front, Engineer Simpson, Supt. Wearing, Lieut. Briggs.
On Engine, standing, Assistant Engineer Wood, Fireman Newsham, Redmayne and Willan. Seated, Fireman Hodgkinson Thompson and Vickers as Driver. Holding the horses Fireman Fletcher.

Lancaster Corporation Transport. The Electric Bus re-charging its batteries in Market Square about 1919. These vehicles had not a long life as the gradients, such as East Road, reduced their speed to less than a walking pace so rendering them unacceptable to the public.

'The Wennington', the first iron Clipper ship built at New Quay Lancaster in 1865. The background is the site of the works of Nairn and Williamson. Over to the left can be seen the Windmill which stood opposite to the present Victoria Hotel, West Road. When you ask a man in Lancaster where he works and he says 'at the Ship Yard' he means at Nairn and Williamsons.

The Landing Sheds, St. Georges Quay. Removed in 1901-2 when the Port Commissioners gave the Quay to the Corporation. St. George's Quay is no longer used by the Commissioners but is gradually being established by the Corporation as an amenity to the Town.

Lancaster old time Fire brigade practicing at the Canal at Dry Dock. In the picture can be seen Chief Constable Harris, Superintendant Wearing, fireman Vickers etc.

LADIES WALK LANCASTER. 27029.

Ladies Walk, now Caton Road, constructed during the 1914-18 War by German Prisoners of War. It is known as King's Way.

The site of the Scotforth Pottery now absorbed into the Hala Road housing estate. The stream, Scotforth or Borough Beck is for some of its length in a culvert. In the field to the right could be seen the clay pits. The tree which was in good condition, was for some obscure reason, cut down when the development took place.

'Oaklea' at the junction of Scotforth Square and Ashford Road. This building erected in 1639 was demolished and replaced by the existing house of the same name in 1898. To the right is the old Scotforth School, now demolished. The man with the basket was known as Owd Bob (Robert Ribchester).

Skerton from Skerton Bridge before the demolition of the houses in recent years. This photograph shows what I pointed out in the introduction that there was and is very little of Old Lancaster that could be preserved other than the good buildings of the Georgian period. Public Health standards made it impossible to perpetuate the life of very few of these buildings.